# DARING MARY
## Aviation Pioneer

MARY SHIPKO

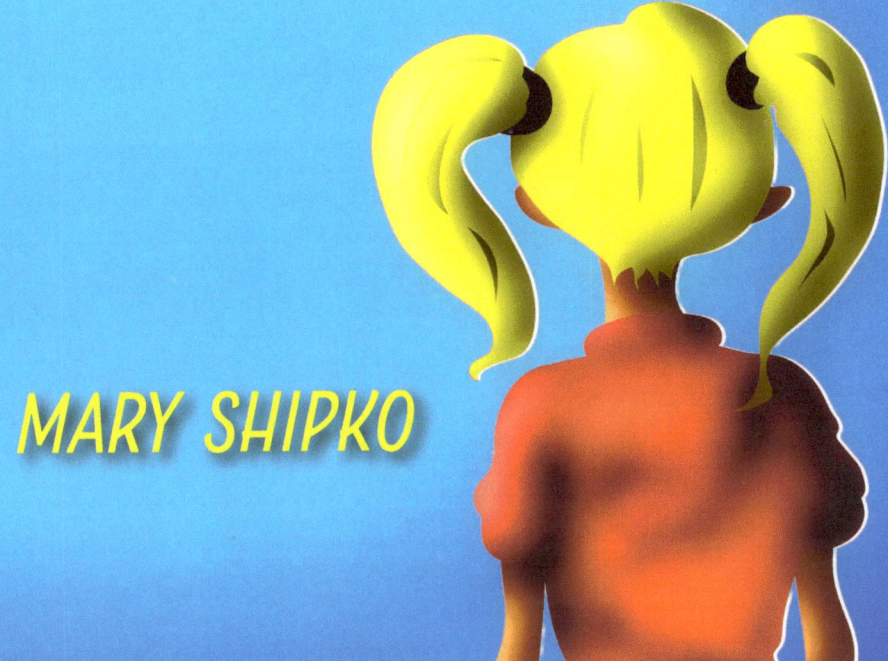

Daring Mary
Aviation Pioneer

Copyright © 2022 by Mary Shipko

ISBNs:
9798985950915 (hardcover)
9798411165883 (paperback)

Published by Shipko Books

All rights reserved. No part of this book may be reproduced or transmitted in any form or by any means without written permission of the author.

In 1955 in Ft Lauderdale, Florida, Mary's brothers were learning to fly.

"To fly, to fly, I must learn too."

But her brothers said "No, only a guy can fly."

"Girls can't fly, don't even try," they yelled.

But, she thought, how can that be?

She would go ask Dad.

Was this true?

"No," said Dad. "You can be anything you want to be".

So she dared to dream of flying in the sky.

Up, up into the sky so blue.

Flying near and far, before she could even drive a car, she dreamed of taking her friends and grandma too.

Early one morning, she spied a seaplane, swooping low over the water.

That night, she dreamed of landing near tiny islands in the sea, and she started to see life differently.

How graceful, Mary thought, when she saw a glider in flight, watching it spiral up, as if a bird in the sky.

That night, in her dreams, she soared.

I must learn to fly!

At sixteen, she finally went to flight school and spread her wings.

She took her plane up high for a solo ride and did loops and spins.

Then she took her friends and grandma too, like she had dreamed to do.

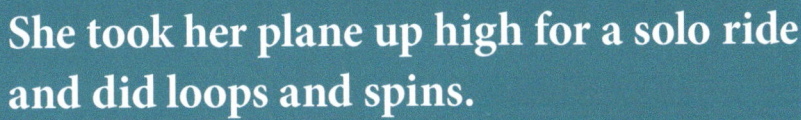

She loved every flight from beginning to end.

A flying job that's what she wanted, she told a friend, she would not bend.

To be a professional pilot she must study hard.

"Now I can go get that flying job" she said.

The Coast Guard needed pilots, the newspaper said.

She wanted to serve her country!

"I'll go see them." she said.

"Oh, no, no," the Coast Guard officer said. "We don't hire women pilots, only brave men to rescue people in trouble."

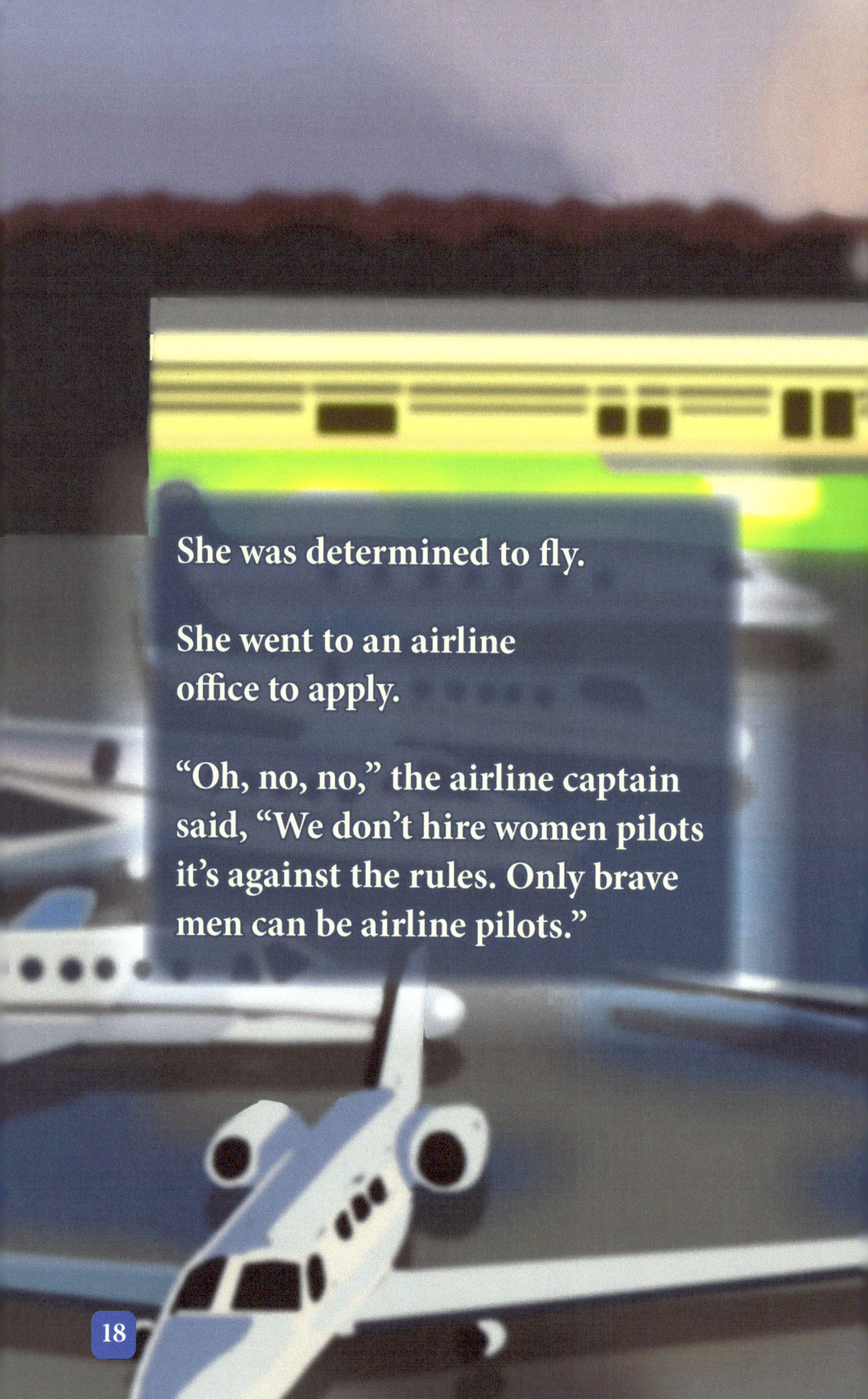

She was determined to fly.

She went to an airline office to apply.

"Oh, no, no," the airline captain said, "We don't hire women pilots it's against the rules. Only brave men can be airline pilots."

She would not give up, so she applied at a small charter company.

"Oh, no, no" the owner said, "We don't hire women pilots here. Our jobs are saved for brave men with families."

"I can be brave too," she thought. Steadfast, she tried again at a cargo company.

"I don't hire women pilots," the owner said. "But today I had a pilot call in sick, I need someone right away. Can you go?"

"Why yes I can," and so, because she didn't give up, she was off on a flying adventure, winging her way to the Caribbean islands.

Then Hurricane Fifi swept through the Caribbean, and Mary was asked to fly a hurricane relief flight. A chance to be brave, she thought.

She was off to Belize, bringing food and clothes, helping people left homeless by the storm.

Rules changed, as they sometimes do, airline companies started to hire women, but only a few.

Mary had held onto her dream, and it finally came true.

Mary was hired as the first woman pilot for Hughes Airwest in 1976 when she was twenty-six years old.

Today, there are over ten-thousand woman airline pilots.

Mary helped open the doors for them.

Her dream came true, how about you?

Turn the page to see how you can become an airline pilot, too.

# How you can become an airline pilot.

Here are the major ways that you can get the education, experience, and training you need to become an airline pilot.

1. The military offers a complete package: education, training, and experience. It is competitive, so start preparing early.

2. A university with an aviation program.

3. A local airport, for flight training. Local clubs like Experimental Aircraft Association (EAA) have programs that offer mentoring, support, and may have a flight program. The Ninety-Nines support young women who are learning to fly. Women in Aviation (WAI) is a great resource also.

4. Some airlines offer assistance with loans, training and job placement. Check with flight schools near you to find out what the current offers are.

5. Get paid to teach others to fly. Become a flight instructor after you attain your commercial rating. Earn your Certified Flight Instructor rating and start teaching others. This is an economical way to build flight time and experience.

# Licenses needed.

**Private pilot certificate.** The first license you get it requires a written test and 40 hours of flight time.

**Commercial certificate.** The second license requires a written test and 250 hours of flight time, divided into 100 hours pilot in command time, 50 hours cross country, and 10 hours with instructor in a complex aircraft. With this license, you can fly for pay.

**Airline Transport Pilot (ATP) certificate.** This is the highest license a pilot can attain. Major airlines require it before getting hired, and regional airlines prefer it. It requires a written test and 1500 hours of flight time.

**Instrument rating.** This is usually earned while working toward the commercial rating. It requires 50 hours of cross-country pilot-in-command and 40 hours of actual or simulated instrument conditions.

**Multi engine.** This is usually earned while working toward the commercial rating.

**Instructor rating.** This is usually earned after the Commercial Rating as a way to pay for building flight time.

# Below are some helpful tips.

1. Start now, read books about aviation, flying, and the lives of pilots. Reading books increases your knowledge and will inspire you. Neil Armstrong, a pilot and the first man on the moon, read over 100 books in first grade, many of them about flying.

2. Be curious and love learning. Pilots are lifelong learners.

3. Become safety-minded. Observe why accidents happen in your home, at school, on the road. Think about how they may have been avoided.

4. Develop situational awareness. It is a good skill and one that you can start learning just around your home. Observe your environment, the activities and events in it and how they interact with you.

5. Develop an interest in technology, science, and math.

6. There are many helpful organizations for a young person wishing to become a pilot. Join one in your area. Experimental aircraft Association, Ninety Nines (99) and Women in Aviation have good programs and they are worth joining.

7. Practice memorization. Flight school requires lots of memorization. Try writing everything down three times, then you will know it by heart.

8. Develop what pilots call a "scan." You can do this at home. Just observe and pay attention to things in your peripheral vision but always come back to your most important job or task at hand.

9. When you start flight lessons always know your heading and airspeed.

10. When you prepare for each lesson, visualize it while sitting in a chair at home. Close your eyes and run through checklists, maneuvers, and performance expectations. Use your imagination to put yourself in a plane soaring through the sky.

Becoming an airline pilot requires a series of licenses, ratings, experience and a college degree. Don't be daunted by the amount of work. It is well worth the effort. Good Luck

# They inspired her.

**Mary's dad** taught her determination and perseverance. When he was 3 years old, he was diagnosed with polio during the 1916 polio epidemic. The doctors told his parents he would never walk again. Thank goodness no one told him. With his leg in a brace, he ran over the farm fields, chasing after his brothers. In a few years, he no longer needed his wheelchair or leg brace, but he had to wear special shoes, and he walked with a slight limp. He was also colorblind, so he could never be an airline or a military pilot, but he did his best at whatever he could, including teaching in the Civilian Pilot Training Program for WWII. Over the course of his life, he taught thousands of people to fly, including Mary. He would always say to her, "Oh nothing that a thousand flight hours won't cure," when Mary would ask how she was doing.. His quiet dignity in the face of almost insurmountable difficulties inspired her.

**Amelia Earhart** was born into a transportation family. Her father was an attorney for a railroad, so they traveled often. She was six years old when the Wright Brothers flew at Kitty Hawk. As a volunteer nurse's aide during WWI, she often cared for young aviators. On her days off, she visited the airport and became enamored with flight. She had a vision of what air transportation could become. As a young woman, she helped to promote aviation through daring flights to unexplored parts of the world, speaking engagements, and working for young airline companies. She lived with courage, fortitude and determination. Mary got to know Amelia through her books, which inspired and challenged her. Amelia said " Women, like men, should try to do the impossible. And when they fail, their failure should be a challenge to others."

## About the Illustrator

Carla Ginsberg is an illustrator and Visual Storyteller, with a BFA from the Fashion Institute of Technology. Her work has been featured from the Fashion Institute of Technology's museum, to art shows around San Francisco. She freelances in book illustration, storyboards, private commissions, teaching art instruction, and businesses. She also owns an animation studio with her husband, where they create videos for companies around the country. Carlas live in Atlanta with her husband and two bunnies Taco and Mimosa. You can view her work at www.carlaginsberg.com and www.visitcistudios.com @carla_paints @_cistudios_

www.ingramcontent.com/pod-product-compliance
Lightning Source LLC
LaVergne TN
LVHW072322080526
838199LV00112B/489